To Lewis, Tyler +

My Aunt Jean's A Dinosaur

Yvonne Ugarte

Love from Yvonne xx

Runcible Spoon Press

First Edition & First published in Great Britain in 2021 by
Runcible Spoon Press,

https://www.runciblespoonpress.co.uk

ISBN 978-1-9161647-3-4

Cover image and My Aunt Jean's a Dinosaur poem illustration: Rebekha Burton

Cover design: David Strafford

Foreword by Yvonne Ugarte

This book contains poems written for my own children and whilst working with primary school children at Beeston Primary School, in Leeds, West Yorkshire England. The poems were written over many years as a means of delighting and teaching children through storytelling.

A huge thank you to all the wonderful children who submitted their artwork and of course, publishers Kathleen & David for believing in me and creating this beautiful book.

The children who contributed to this book were:

Finley Ahern, Emaan Ali, Kacie Temple-Baker, Tamina Barati, Peyton Buckley, Faith Burton, Olive Bromley, Malado Camara, Caleb Cartledge, Amelia Clegg, Ruby Costello, Olivia Crawford, Sienna Garbutt, Riha Garside, Jack Hammil, Olivia Harker, Thomas Hedley, Indi Hewitt, Lexi Hoban, Mason Horncastle, Manha Hoque, Naomi Iorga, Sara Karem, Khadija Khan, Leon Kitching, Kiara Knowles, Jasmine Kolopovica, Lily Mae Millard, Megan O'Grady, Hannah Phelan, Holly Phelan, Juno Poules, Anzara Sabbir, Joel Scopes, Rose Shilliday, Aurora Smith, Emily Smith, Maria Yolande-Sorgho, Leon Tinker, Amali Ugarte, Chloe Varley, Vincent McHale-Webster, Daria Zevzikova

All proceeds from the sale of this book will be donated to Martin House Hospice who treated my son with dignity, love and support.

To my son, *Emil Sebastian Ugarte* who inspired many of these poems.

Contents

My Aunt Jean's A Dinosaur

I know Aunt Jean's a dinosaur,
but no-one else agrees.
What else would have such scaly skin and fat
enormous knees?

And on her back I've seen a ridge that runs
along her spine,
they're like those plates on Stegosaurs
from Prehistoric times.

I've seen her eat a chicken whole with rows of
sharp
white teeth.
Her skirt sticks out an awful lot - is that a tail
beneath?
Her hands are huge with nails like claws,
her two long ears stick out.
Is my Aunt Jean a dinosaur?
She is - I have no doubt!

Cat

His amber eyes were half
closed.
Huge, pink padded paws
tucked beneath his chin.
Long squirrel-brush tail
twitching oh so gently.
He saw his human enter the
room.
He knew the name of his
slave.
He lazily rolled over,
a low purr escaping
from his exposed throat.
She bent down and
spoke in a soft voice,
extending a friendly hand
towards him.
His mellow, amber eyes
instantly turned to black,
and a snarl curled his lip.
Too late she withdrew her
hand.
First blood was his!

Friends

My classmate Keith has no
front teeth,
and Lloyd has a wonky nose.
Gill has ears like
cauliflowers,
and Ann has turned-in toes.
I've got freckles all over my
face,
and the knobbliest knees
you've seen.
But we still have giggles
and lots of fun.
We're the best
friends there's ever
been!

Pets

My friend thinks that pets
are disgusting.
"Just look at the trouble they
cause!"
If you're going away
where will Bunnykins stay?
Who'll get rid
of the straw
from her
paws?

My friend thinks that pets
are disgusting,
when they whimper and
whine for their food,
and their breath's far from
sweet,
when they've
gobbled their
meat,
and the noise from
their bottoms is rude!

My friend
thinks that pets are
disgusting,
'cos they piddle and poo on
the floor,
and the budgies I keep
make her eyes itch and weep,
and go running away
through the door.

My friend thinks all pets are
disgusting.
They select certain humans
to tease.
They then play a game
where they terrorise Jane
with their claws and their
bites and their fleas!

My friend thinks all pets are disgusting.

Says she's not met a pleasant one yet.
It's a plot they all hatch where they slither and scratch,
and it's HER that they all seem to get!

My friend thinks all pets are disgusting.
If she could, she would send them all back!
Her biggest pet-hate,
is my big sister's snake
and the mice that it eats as a snack.

My friend thinks all pets are disgusting,
how they slobber and follow her round.
They jump up and they nip
and they make her feel sick,
hopes they get lost and never are found.

My friend thinks all pets are disgusting.
Said she'd NEVER have one in her house,
but I know that Jane lied
there's a fish-tank inside,
and a rumour she has a pet mouse...

I Cannot Write A Poem

I cannot write a poem
because the sky is just too
blue.
I'm thinking, now, of
playtime, and the things I
want to do.
I cannot write a
poem because my
shoe lace is
undone,
and the boy who's
sitting next to me is
popping bubble-gum.
I cannot write a poem
because my words
just never rhyme,
and now my
teacher's packing up
because it's dinner
time.

I cannot write a poem
because I'm jumping on the
wall,
the dinner lady's telling me
to stop in case I fall.
I cannot write a poem
because I tripped and
bumped my head.
I should be thinking what to
write, but I'm stuck inside
instead.
I cannot write a
poem because
my pencil's on
the floor,
and my teacher's
closely watching me,
he's standing by the
door.
I cannot write a poem
because it's now the
end of school,

but wait...I think this poem does work!
How brill, how neat! how cool!

Time Lapse

I turned the key to the hidden room
and pushed the door aside.
The sun streamed in to breathe new life
to memories long since died.

With child-like thrill I touched the toys
that long forgotten lay.
A rocking horse stood in the midst,
its colours brightly gay.

The sun alone bedecked its form
no dust to dim its hue.
It stood apart from all the rest
with paint as good as new.

With cautious step, I ventured near
though fear within me stirred.
The horse began to slowly rock,
then children's voices heard.

I felt them pass but could not see
their presence real and strong.
One climbed upon the rocking horse
their timeless souls lived on.

A stranger, I, within their world
where I'd no right to be,
I locked the door and walked away
then threw away the key.

Summer

Summer has arrived now
and so has the sun.
Fingers of warmth
fall on everyone.
Splash on the sun-cream
get plenty to drink
to nourish our brains
make it better to think.
It's almost break-up time
so teachers can rest,
no phonics or
Maths.
Oh yes, Summer's
the best!

The Lion Who Lost His Roar

Leonard Lion stretched and yawned,
combed out his lion-cub mane.
He ate his breakfast,
brushed his teeth,
and splashed in summer rain.
He saw a snail and tried to growl,
but found no sound arose!
He tried again by standing on one leg
with both eyes closed.
He even stood upon his head
did cartwheels all around,

he jumped across the stream three times,
but STILL he made no sound.
Nigel monkey called to him
from a branch up in the tree,
"I can help you, little cub,
but you need to follow me.
I know an owl within a cave
and she will help for sure.
She keeps a box with all lost noises in,
she'll find your roar!"
Lorna Owl lives many miles
from our leafy jungle home.
But I'll go with you, little cub,
so you won't feel so alone.
Leonard lion-cub thanked his friends and set off straight away. His paws were sore,

his eyes abrim with tears he
wiped away.
How strange those sounds
that filled his ears,
as the sunshine hid from
view.
Dark clouds gathered all
around
those
weary,
sleepy
two.
The
stars

were shining brightly
when they both reached
Lorna's cave.
And when they heard her
screeching hoots
they did not feel so brave!

The cave was dark and then
she fluttered into view,
her orange eyes glared down
at them,
then she blinked, as all owls
do.
Nigel monkey told her why
they'd travelled
all that way,
and how the little lion-cub
had lost his roar that day.
"Come with me and let me
see if I can find your roar,

just promise not to use it to
scare small things anymore."
They followed her along the
trail
that led to a moonlit space.
Perched on high, her
talons held,
a wooden box in place.
She raised the lid and many
sounds
were waiting to be found!
Croaks of frogs, the moos of
cows,
the barking of a hound.
He swallowed hard and
fought back tears,
as he searched the box again.
Howls of foxes, the baas of
lambs
and the cluckity cluck of
hens.
With a heavy heart, young
Leonard
searched the box just like
before.
And at the very bottom of it
lay his mighty roar!
So happy he, he jumped with
glee,
"Oh, thank you, my dear
friends!"
And back they went to his
jungle home,
now he'd found his roar
again.
He remembered what the
owl had said,
and the promise that he
made.
He didn't use his roar for fun
or make creatures feel afraid.
So if YOU ever lose your
voice,

don't worry it won't be
found.
Just stand on one leg and
close your eyes
and turn three times around.

A Child's Place

Give me a child
with a mind of
their own. Show
me the one in the
corner alone,
the one in reception who still
misses mum,
who still wants a cuddle
along with the fun.
Give me
some
paper,
we'll all
make a
boat
with crayons &
some folding - hey presto!
They float! Books for all
ages and clothes in the den,
a new Mrs Doubtfire or just
Mister Benn?

A corner for homework, to
think and to study
or games in the playground
(be careful, it's muddy!).
Lunch in the hall or a pack-
up instead,
puddings and fruit to ensure
they're well fed.
For those who
are quiet
and want
their own
space,
we've a
nurture
room & areas to chill at their
own pace.
We're a child-centred school,
so tuned in to pupil's needs,
we are Beeston Primary, and
proud to be from Leeds.

Snow Leopard And Friends

Young Larry the leopard
climbed down from his tree,
"I'm bored with the jungle -
there's not much to see!
I've heard of a land that is
covered in snow,
with icebergs and penguins
and cool winds that blow.
That's where I will visit!" he
said with a grin,
"I want to taste
snowflakes, feel ice
on my
chin.
And if it's too
cold, I can always
come back
- now where is my
suitcase?" he cried,
"I must pack! "
He mapped out his journey
and carefully planned,
the route he would take over
mountains and sands.
Not wanting to wait, having
made up his mind,
he said his goodbyes, left the
jungle behind.
It took many
moons 'til at last
he was there,
a land of strange
magic,

with cool, frosted air.
He created a leopard from
out of the snow
and together they played,
making snowballs to throw.

He told his new friend of his
life in the sun,
"I'd like you to visit one
day...will you come?
You'll meet all my family, my
special friends too.
We'll go hunting and
climbing like REAL leopards
do!"
"I'd love to go meet them!"
the snow leopard said,
"I'll hunt and I'll play, climb
the trees to your bed.
I might become covered in
spots, just like you.
Oh yes, Larry Leopard,
please take me there too!"
So Larry agreed with a nod
of his head
"But first you must hear of
the dangers," he said.
"We'll stay one more week
here before we return
for the climate back home
has a sun that will burn.
So be warned!" Larry added,
"The heat there is strong
and your skin is so pale so
we mustn't stay long."
The day soon arrived when
they headed for home,
through meadows and
streams did those weary
friends roam.
The sun was quite high when
they entered a wood,
and the snow leopard
groaned, "I'm not feeling too
good..."
He cried when describing the
way that he felt,
"Oh Larry, I'm shrinking! I'm
starting to melt!"
And Larry looked down at
the pool by his feet,
"I warned you before of this
sweltering heat.

The snow in my suitcase has
already gone
So we won't reach the jungle,
the sunshine's too strong!"
"We'd better turn back then,"
the snow leopard said,
"You tell all your family
about me instead.
For I can live only where
coldest winds freeze
- I'd never survive in your
jungle of trees.
So bring your friends with
you the next time you come,
we'll make more snow
creatures and really have
fun!"
And so Larry joined his new
friend in the snow,
along with his friends who
had begged him to go.
And living out there on the
ice, cool and bright,
they each found their coats
turning gradually white.
So Larry, Sam Stoat, Freddy
Fox and Hank Hare,
became Arctic creatures and
still live out there.
If thoughts turn to meadows,
or jungles with streams,
they just close their eyes and
return in their dreams...

Gordon Grizzly

Gordon Grizzly was a
grumpy bear with eyes of
steely green,
to grown-ups he was the real
scare-bear,
with a snarl that was low and
mean.
He had a scar on his big, fat
tum,
sharp claws at the end of his
paws.
His nose was black and his
ears were small,
and 42 teeth in his jaws.

But none of the children
were ever afraid.
They knew he was
misunderstood.
Gordon's grumpiness ends
when he plays with his
friends,
he is lovely and cuddly and
good.

Fantasy Football

I can't believe it's
football on each
channel
one, two, three
why can't there be another
kind
especially for me?
Caterpillar hockey-players,
flea rugby against ants,
or basketball with earwigs
wearing 6-legged
underpants?
Tai Kwando with crocodiles
or ballet dancing
dogs,
rhinos playing
cricket,
scoring runs against
the frogs.
Football IS important

and of that I will agree,
but must it be a human
that should be the
referee?
Spiders make
good linesmen,
for with eight
eyes would surely see,
that offside goal the tiger
shot,
and the injured hippo's knee.
If an octopus was goalie,
how could England fail to
win?
Eight long arms would surely
stop those goals from getting
in...

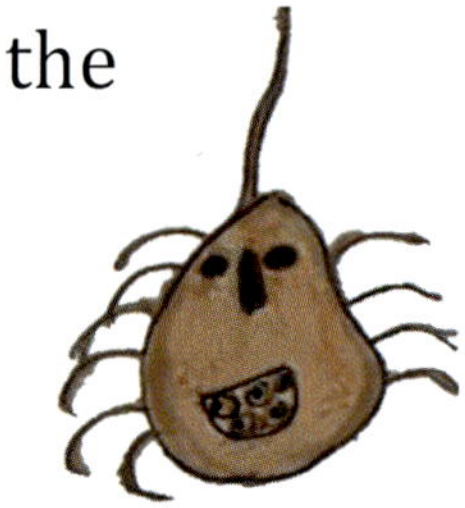

Poles Apart

Penguins live in Antarctica,
(The South Pole to you and me).
But Polar bears live in the Arctic,
so they'd NEVER meet up for tea!
The Antarctic hosts the Albatross,
elephant seals and even snails!
But the Walrus lives in the Arctic,
like the puffin and Beluga whales.
The Antarctic is land that's surrounded by sea,
and it's colder, with icebergs and caps.
The Arctic is sea surrounded by land,
so the animals learn to adapt.
The Arctic has winters from October to March.
The Antarctic from March to September,
penguins and polar bears live Poles apart,
and that's all that you need to remember...

Talk To Me

My upside
down
smile
means I
might need
a friend.
Come and
sit with
me.
The school day seems so long
when I am lonely.
Let me join in your games if I
want to.
Talk to me.
Take time out to listen to the
words I find hard to say.

Please don't walk away.
Ask me how my day has
been.
Be my friend.

Smile at me. Talk to me.
Listen to me.
If you see me standing alone
at the edge of the
playground, do not walk past
me.
Ask me how I am feeling.
Do not make me feel
invisible.
Talk to me.
I just might need a friend.
A friend like you,
so STOP !
Talk to me.
Listen to my small voice.
Don't just leave me standing
there.
Stand next
to me.
Be my
friend.
And show
me you
care.

Arnold Armadillo

Arnold armadillo twitched
his long and snuffly nose.

He scratched his floppy ears
with his sharp and scaly toes.
He heard a scary noise and
so he rolled up in a ball,

so tightly did he roll
himself, he had no
face at all!

The other
creatures left
him there,
they
wouldn't let
him play.

He was just so shy they
passed him by, he was lonely
every day.

When Arnold spoke, his little
voice was very hard to hear,

so by the time he'd told
them how he felt, they'd
disappeared!

But Arnold
armadillo wasn't
fazed by this at
all,

he'd eat the
termites that he
found then curl
up in a ball.

Munch

Once upon a yum-yum time,
I knew a cow called Munch.
She drank elderberry
milkshakes,
and ate pineapples for lunch.
Her face was white and
purple,
but her body was bright
green.
The most amazing yum-yum
cow
that I had ever seen.
She had three
little rabbit friends,
called Nibble, Bite and Chew.
Nibble was like a poodle
but with spots of brightest
blue.
Bite looked like a zebra
stripy fur with eyes of red.

They'd all been friends
forever,
in the yum-yum books they
read.
Chew looked like a billy-goat
with purple fur and horns.
Along with Munch they
played
among the daffodils and
thorns.

yum
yum

Noah's Ark

Noah got a message from the
Heavenly Lord above,
He said, "Prepare your
family, cos there's going to
be a flood!
I want you all to hear me for
you have to build a boat

to save you all from
drowning and to keep
yourselves afloat.

Build a floating reptilarium,
aquarium and zoo,
to fill it, you must bring back
every creature, two by two,
from buffaloes to
butterflies, baboons to
hissing snakes,
for these you must protect
from death when darkest
heaven breaks.

You and all your family will
be saved to live anew.
But first I must destroy the
earth to rid the evil too.
Because of your belief in
me, the goodness in your
heart,

it's up to you to build for me
this enterprising Ark

That's a floating reptilarium,
aquarium and zoo,
filled with all the creatures
you've collected, two by two,
from buffaloes to butterflies,
baboons to hissing snakes,

and these you will protect
from death when darkest
heaven breaks.
For forty days and forty
nights the rains shall swell
the sea,
and all the life created for my
world will cease to be.

And after this, a raven must
be sent into the skies.
If he returns, then stay afloat,
the seas have yet to rise.

Stay in your floating
reptilarium, aquarium and
zoo,
with all the other creatures
you've collected, two by two,
from buffaloes to
butterflies, baboons to
hissing snakes,
for these you will
protect from death as
darkest heaven
breaks.

A week must pass before you
send a dove to scan the sea.

If she brings back an olive
branch, it's there your home
shall be.
And I will send a rainbow
that will shine across your
land,
but know that all this comes
to you by my Almighty hand.

So leave your floating
reptilarium, aquarium and
zoo.
Put back all the creatures
you've collected two by two.
The buffaloes to butterflies,
baboons to hissing snakes,
to climb the trees and
swim the seas and fly
across the lakes."

Alliteration Animals

Anxious armadillos
bumbling, buzzing bugs
clambering, climbing, curious cats
dizzy, dancing ducks.
Eight enormous elephants
funny, fish-faced frogs
giggling, gaggling, gaping geese
happy, hairy hogs.
Itchy iguanas
jackal's jelly jam,
karate kicking kangaroos
lolly-licking lamb.
Monkeys making music,
nightjar's noisy nest.
Overbearing octopus
petulant, pelican pest.
Quarrelsome, quirky quail chicks,
rhino's raging rush.
Sixteen slithering serpents,

tortoise-tickling thrush.
Undulating unicorn fish
vocal vipers vexed.
Wriggly, wiggly, wiry worm
X-ray Xerus X.
Yodelling, Yorkshire, youthful yak,
and now you'll clearly see.
The last one in this animal list
Is zany, zebra Zebedee

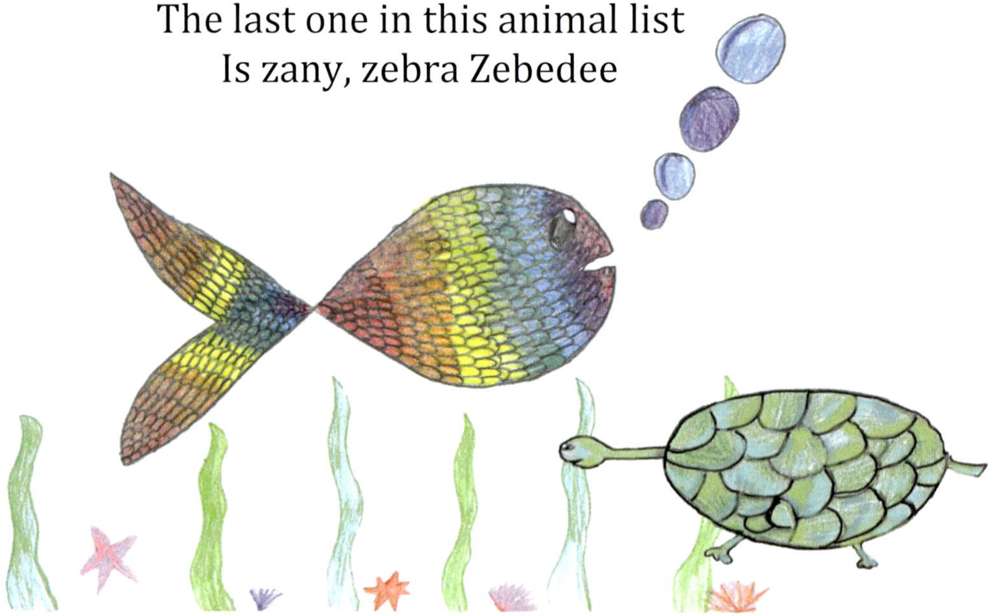

Minnie Mouse

Minnie the mouse lives here,
under the stairs.
She runs through
the kitchen and
clambers on
chairs.
She gobbles
up crumbs
that we've dropped on the
floor,
then darts past the table and
back through the door.
She's small, brown and furry
and not at all fat,
she likes all our family
EXCEPT for our cat!
She never comes out if old
Smokey is near,
with whiskers a tremble, she
cowers in fear.
But Smokey won't chase her
- he's too old to run.
He'd rather sprawl out on
the grass in the sun.
He can't even see her, he'd
just pounce in vain.
Old Smokey will never go
hunting again.
But Minnie's still wary,
though I tempt her with
cheese.
Yet all I can hear is the shake
of her knees!
If Smokey
walks past,
she will stick
out her
tongue,
but she
won't leave
her hole 'til
she's certain
he's gone.

Ballerina

She runs on the stage, her
feet perfectly poised,
like a statue of
silver she stands.

To a round of
applause
uncontrollably loud,
she begins, with a
stroke of her
hands.
How perfect she is
for a young
ballerina.
with tutu of satin,
snow white.
Her stance so majestic,
the slippers she wears, as
herself, are so magic, so light!

Gliding and dancing she
floats through the air.
Pirouettes are
performed with such
style!
This lady of grace with
the angel-like face,
wins us all with her
beautiful smile.
So slowly she spins as she
touches the floor,
takes her leave amidst
deafening applause.
The music then fades as the
curtains are closed,
and she exits alone through
the doors.

The Three Little Sheep

The first little sheep was
poor, and he built his house
of straw,
so when the wolf came along,
with a dance and a song,
breakfast was what he saw!
"Little sheep, little sheep - let
me come in,
I'll show you how
to dance, I'll
show you how
to sing!
PLEASE let me in!"
But the little sheep
knew that the wolf
wasn't true,
and he wouldn't unlock
the door.

"Okay!" said the wolf, "Then
I'll huff. I'll puff and I'll huff
and I'll puff!"
Then he said with a frown, "I
will blow your house down,
and my tummy will be full
today!"
So he huffed and he puffed,
and he puffed and he huffed,
and he blew the little straw
house down!
So the little sheep ran (as
only little sheep can)
to his brother's
house, two miles
away.
Now the second
little sheep used
wood and he
covered it up
with mud.
So when the wolf came
along, with a dance and a
song,

he said what all little clever
sheep should!
"Go away, Mister Wolf, go away - we don't want you round here today.
'Cos we know how to sing and we know how to dance, so you'd better be on your way!"
"Okay!" said the wolf, "Then I'll huff, I'll puff and I'll huff and I'll puff!"
Then he said with a frown, "I will blow your house down, and my tummy will be full today!"
So he huffed and he puffed and he puffed and he huffed,
and he blew the little wooden house down!

Now the little sheep ran (as only little sheep can) to their brother's house, three miles away.
Now the third little sheep used brick - it was solid, it was wide, it was thick.
So when the wolf came along with a dance and a song,
he was angry and he waved a big stick.
"Go home, Mister Wolf, go home! We just want you to leave us alone!
We're not scared anymore 'cos this house is secure,
'cos I built it with bricks and stone."
"Okay!" said the wolf, "Then I'll huff, I'll puff and I'll huff and I'll puff!"
Then he said with a frown, "I will blow your house down, and my tummy will be full today!"

So he huffed and he puffed,
he puffed and he huffed,
but he couldn't blow the
brick house down.
He tried many ways 'til his
head was in a daze,
but he STILL couldn't
blow the house
down.
Then a chimney he
spied on the house.
So he crept up as quiet as
a mouse.
Down inside he could see all
the sheep were having tea!
He was as angry as a wolf
could be!
Then the wolf tried to climb
down inside,
thinking how he'd give them
all a big surprise.
But he was so full of ire he
just didn't see the fire

'til it burnt his paw...and oh,
how he cried!
Now the three little sheep
felt sad,
though they knew that the
wolf was bad.
So they bandaged up his
paw (which was very,
very sore)
and let him stay to
share the yummy tea
they had.
Now the wolf, when he'd
eaten all the tea,
was as grateful as a wolf
could be.
He drank his milk in little
sips,
ate more cake then licked his
lips
and ate up ALL the little
sheepies, one, two, three!

Yum!

There was an old
woman who
swallowed a fly.
She liked her fast food,
thought she'd give it a try!
First, she ate wings
and then she
tried feet,
greenfly and
midges all went
down a treat.

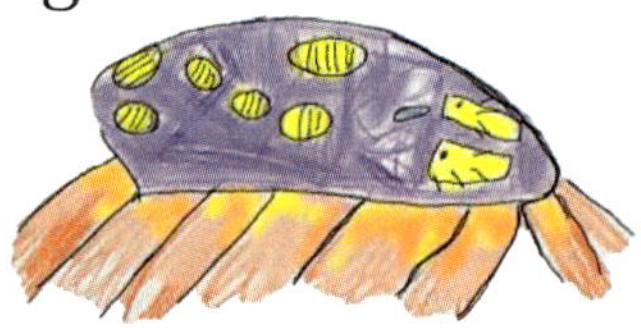

Beetles were crunchy and
ants tasted funny,
moths were quite dry but
their insides were runny!
Earwigs and horseflies,
hornets and bees,
ladybirds, lacewings then
head lice and fleas.
The one she liked best was
the wasp on the wing.
She'd bite off his head, keep
his sting in a tin.
An adrenaline junkie, scaling
up cliffs,
for sand flies and weevils,
mosquitoes and thrips.
The last I had heard, she had
gone to Brazil,
to eat giant water bugs
(The ultimate thrill)!
But her tantalised taste
buds
never savoured her goal,
for a huge anaconda came
and ate her up whole!

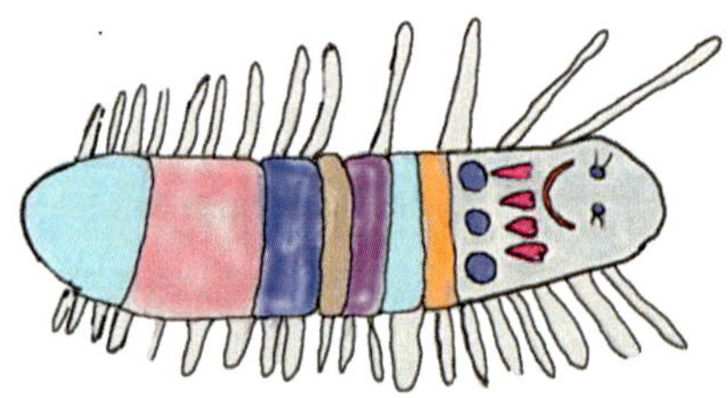

Dino Wood

I once saw a dinosaur while shopping with my mum.

It waddled up the frozen aisle with its big,
enormous bum.
It grabbed three packs of frozen peas and tossed them in the air,
thundered past the check-out girl as if she wasn't there!
It didn't count on Brenda Wood, on duty by the door,

(She's the tough security guard who helps protect the store)!
That dinosaur looked quite surprised as Brenda roared
"GOODBYE!"

She grabbed its tail and flung it out - she made that dino fly!
It landed with a heavy thump and blocked the whole main road.
But Brenda hadn't finished yet and over there she strode,
with a grumpy face, she clenched her fist and socked it on its jaw,
snatched those packs of frozen peas it still had in its claws.
"NO-ONE STEALS FROM BILLY'S STORE!" she shouted, really loud.
And all we heard were claps and cheers from a quickly growing crowd.
The Journalists and TV crews praised Brenda, as they should.
And now the park across the road's been re-named
DINO WOOD!

The Awakening

The hedgehog rouses from
her slumber,
her quills moistened by
droplets of dew.
Nose twitching, she trundles
through the sleeping forest.
Fingers of warmth from a
hazy sun
heralding the birth of a new
day.
The owl sleeps on,
this silent assassin of
razor claw and sharp
eye,
nocturnal
ninja with
superhero sonar.
Her owlets dream with full
bellies,
in a nest lined with the fur of
their prey.

Blackbird pauses from his
melodious song,
his black, orange-ringed eye
surveys,
the leaf littered floor for a
whisper of movement.
Coal-tar wings
flutter
effortlessly
from his
branch,
as he swoops,
his gold-
dipped beak
stabs at the
rustling
creatures beneath his feet.
His diligent patience
rewarded with a beak
abrim with insects to feed his
yellow-mouthed brood.
And thus the forest awakens.

Vic The Veggie Spider

I'm Vic the
veggie
spider,
I don't eat
living things.
Give me
wheat or grass or
rye,
not things with legs or wings.

My 99 brothers and sisters
all make webs, catch bugs
and flies,
they hide green fly in my
food
but I see through their
disguise!

I have to say it's a lonely life.
my invites to parties have
fallen.

From the moment they see I
don't eat winged meat,
my family and friends have
stopped calling.

I try to make friends with the
things in my web,
the midges, the moths and
the flies,
but when I release them,
they simply fly off,
they all think that I'm just
spinning lies!

But today, by the stream, I
was nibbling on fruit,
when a beautiful spider
dropped in.
She looked at me warmly
with 8 lovely eyes,
and that's where our
friendship begins.

This arachnid I met was a
veggie one too,
she offered me fangs full of
rice,
"My name is Jan –
I'm so glad we're the same,
there's no need to eat beetles
or flies!"

Pandora

Pandora knew when
she got the box,
the message was
perfectly clear.

"THIS MUST NOT BE
OPENED! IT MUST REMAIN
CLOSED!"

But the foolish girl's heart
knew no fear.
And when the key turned, a
green smoke then appeared,
the silly girl should've
known then,
that in opening the box
something dreadful would
come,
and it couldn't be closed up
again.

Out of it came every horror
on earth!
Illness and sadness and
tears,
poverty, pestilence, misery
untold,
anger and sorrow and fears.
Pandora cried out as this evil
escaped
to wreak havoc all over the
world.
Oh, what a tragedy! How she
did cry,
foolish, unfortunate girl!
But then came a noise from
the base of the box,
and a gentle and sweet voice
then said,
"My power is HOPE - I can
help to control
all the evil and menace now
spread."

Today there exists many bad
things on earth,
from the moment she
opened that box.
But hope still remains in
each corner of earth,
ensuring that all is not lost.

Jurassic Nightmare

Poor Delilah dinosaur!
She'd slept right through the time.
All her kind had vanished
from the evolutionary line.
So when she woke, her little world,
was not as it had been.
A concrete jungle
had replaced
the plains and misty stream.
She didn't know what
humans were,
had never seen a house,
and when she saw a car, she bolted
squeaking like a mouse!
Her giant heart was pounding
as she hid behind some trees,

she couldn't hide the falling tears,
or stop her quaking knees.
Poor Delilah dinosaur
felt lost and all alone.
She'd lost her friends and family
and she couldn't find
her home.
She cried herself to
sleep that night
afraid at all she'd
seen.
Then woke to find it
wasn't real!
She'd only had a dream.
But when she told her family
what she feared
they all cried, "Never!
No wheels on tins or two-legged things 'cos we'll exist
forever!"

Did You Know?

Humpty Dumpty didn't fall,
I think you should be told!
'Cos he was pushed right off
that wall
by a grumpy Old King Cole.

And little Miss Muffet who
ran from her tuffet?
Well, that isn't strictly true.
'Cos Horace the spider was
really her friend.
She was startled by Little
Boy Blue!

And Mary Mary Quite
Contrary?
Well, I have to beg your
pardon.
'Cos she couldn't grow a
mustard seed
let alone a garden!